Cont

Early Reviews
Introduction
The Fundamentals of Strategy and Tactics
Your Entry Into Tennis Strategy
Strategy One: Get and Keep the Ball in Play
Tactics For Servers "Keep the Ball In Play"
Tactics for Returners "Keep the Ball in Play"
Tactics In a Rally "Keep the Ball in Play"
Match Day - Keep the Ball in Play
Strategy Two: Pressure Opponent's Movement
Directional Shots Pressure Opponent's Movement
Depth Control for Advancing Players
Match Day Pressuring Your Opponent's Movement
Strategy Three: Pressure Your Opponent's Time and Space
Subtle and Obvious Tactics to Pressure Time and Space
Best Pressure Tactic
2nd Best Pressure Tactic
Match Day Pressure Time and Space
Strategy Four: Break Up Your Opponent's Rhythm
Tactics for Breaking Up Opponent's Rhythm
Match Day Break Up Opponent's Rhythm
Strategy Five: Overpower your Opponent
Match Day: Power Strategy
The Best and Most Tiring Ways to Win
Changing Strategy Mid Match
Building New Strategy Into Your Game
Developing a Long Term Approach to Playing Style

The Fundamentals of Strategy and Tactics

To fully understand strategy, we also need to understand how tactics fit or do not fit with the strategy you may have chosen. Note the Venn Diagram (you may want to explain that to the readers – or show a picture) and inside of the larger circle Strategy are three smaller circles tactic 1, tactic 2 and tactic 3. Also note that tactic 4 is outside the circle.

To add some flesh and bones to what is written here I will tell a short story to illustrate the point of strategy and tactics:

Tactics that Fit a Strategy

Shreyas had a tough match looming, He had recently become a full time serve and volley player; he had not yet fully gained confidence in his ability to beat a top player using this new strategy exclusively. He was worried about an upcoming sectional tournament match, because the opponent had incredible topspin groundstrokes and seemed to really love to hit passing shots more than anything. As is true of some players, the opponent enjoyed having a target at the net to sharpen his focus. So we put our heads together, and came up with the 'kitchen sink' strategy of working very hard to disrupt the rhythm of the opponent. Knowing that players with heavy topspin games feature power and placement require one thing: a relatively consistent ball coming to them so they can time their shot. Shreyas' job on the day would be to completely mix things up and destroy the possibility of his opponent developing any consistency. As a side note, this is one reason why I don't like when players say, "I need to be more consistent", because it can actually play right into the hands of your opponent.

The 'kitchen sink' is my colloquial expression for using a disruptive strategy and it consists of every shot you can think of to hit. Essentially, it means hitting no two shots alike. The strategy was maximum rhythm disruption, and the tactics were to hit the ball: Fast then slow, high then low, more Spin, less Spin, opposite Spin, cross court, down the line, up the middle. The tactic that was NOT in the strategy was to rally consistently or try to out hit the opponent.

Shreyas did very well and winning the first set while surprising his opponent with the strategy. His opponent seemed to blame himself for playing poorly, but we knew that it was the effect of strategy that was beating him. Then Shreyas almost made a fateful ongoing mistake. For three games in the second set he went away from the strategy, using tactics that did not fit the strategy. He began to 'hit' with the opponent, giving him the consistently powerful shots that work well for him, the opponent won those three games very quickly. Those 3 games seemed like they were over in less than 10 minutes and a momentum shift had occurred in the match. The opponent won the second set due to this turnabout. However, Shreyas went back to the original tactics that fit within the strategy of disruption, winning the match convincingly in the third set. One of the most valuable aspects of the high school tennis experience is that a coach can remind the player about the game plan and help get them back on track. This gives the player a better tennis education, one that they can use in future matches.

When selecting a strategy, be sure that the tactics you select are in line with that same strategy. I also encourage you to remain open minded, because you may discover a shot or a sequence that works on that day in that match, so you can include that in your game plan. Be aware changes to your tactics that support or do not support your strategy, then manage them moving forward. Finally if you are down a set and a break, you either need to play much better, or switch to plan B. I have seen quite a few matches where a player has chosen the current game plan, and is down a set and break and either elevates their level of play, or the game plan begins to take a cumulative effect on the opponent and will now be truly effective and lead to the best chance of victory. The rest of this book will breakdown a menu of game plans: A, B, C, D, and E, but you can order them in any way you choose, but they must fit with your current skill set. If your skill set is limiting you, get out and take a lesson. Build your game one lesson at a time.

#

Your Entry into Tennis Strategy

As you look at some of the foundations of Tennis strategy, consider your skill set. You can enter this system at any of the five entry points, these are the different game plans A, B, C, D, E. Here is where you will take the list and put it in the order that works for you best. From there it's up to you which of the other four you want to explore and expand on to develop a B, and a C game. Very few people can effectively work all five of the strategies contained herein, but you will win many more matches if you at least have a B game to shift to in time of need. So, let's take a look at some foundational truths of tennis strategy. This eBook was inspired by a parent with whom I was discussing 'A comprehensive book' on strategy. She asked "Will it cover the basics?", to which I said "Of course". At which point I made a mental note to cover the basics. However, just because these things are basic, does not necessarily make them easy. Later, this book will become part of a compilation with all my other works on strategy into one large print book which will be available in 2015.

The Hierarchy of How To Win Points, or At Least Not Lose Them Easily

When first learning Tennis take these following concepts in order from most basic to the most advanced:
   1. Get the ball in play, even if you have to lob, or bunt the ball back.
   2. Choose a direction, down the line, cross court or down the middle.
   3. Hit to a direction and to the depth that you choose (deep/short, short/deep shot combinations can be deadly).
   4. Choose a spin. This hierarchy differs from Match Play and the Spin of the Ball,where Bill Tilden (Match Play and the Spin of the Ball) states "Every ball must be hit with some type of intentional spin"
   5. Using the Speed of Your Shot or Power Tennis.

The training of players for power and speed and where it fits on the list is subject to great debate. Suffice it to say that if you can overpower your opponent without dramatically increasing your errors, you should do it. The full range of thought on this is varies extremely from: "Hit it as hard as you can, until it starts to go in" and "Play like a man or woman" to "Control and accuracy are what the game is really about, and you would suffer a temporary loss of those while learning incrementally more power, so for now just keep it in". You can also intentionally change speeds on your shots.Those that say that powerful tennis is the only effective tennis, might say that the ceiling of what can be achieved with power will be diminished if you are preoccupied with control in your developmental stages. The other group would say that you may lose confidence early if you lose a lot of matches by playing a high risk game, while other young players are playing in a very controlled fashion early on in their tennis career. It can be instructive to us, that the players who are very successful in the younger age ranges are not usually very successful in the older age ranges when more power is rewarded more often. Young kids under age 12 lack power, so they can win with a keep it in style, later they will be beaten by players who have mastered one of the other four strategies. The question becomes, what is your strategy for now, and which strategy do you want to develop in your game? As a coach, I expose my players to every strategy available.

Strategy One: Get and Keep the Ball in Play

The most important aspect of Tennis is getting and keeping the ball in play. This does not mean necessarily mean 'be consistent', because being consistent may mean putting the ball in play in a way that your opponent really loves. The phrase 'be consistent' is far too non-specific, and usually leads to unreasonable expectations in regard to how often a player can put the ball in play. I have never heard a player come off the court saying, "I was happy with my consistency today". How can we make this instruction more specific, so as to be helpful?

When getting the ball in play, work hard to avoid your opponent's favorite shot, or you will find it very difficult to keep the in play, if you are constantly under attack. Once I had the chance to coach a high ranked junior player while helping a high school coach, because I wanted to be helpful. The high ranked junior who should have been much more intelligent kept saying, "I need to be more consistent". My message to her was "You can keep the ball away from the opponent's preferred strike zone.", to which she responded "I feel like I need to be more consistent". I tell that story to underscore what has become a not very thoughtful approach to the game with consistency.

You can work very hard to keep the ball to toward the outside edges of the court. Another thing to consider is the question "Who is the better player at making angled shots in this match?" If it's you, then by all means make some angled shots, however if it's your opponent, then you may want to direct more balls deep down the center of the court. Be sure to hit the ball deep when you hit down the middle of the court, because if you drop the ball in the center of the court every time, your opponent will have a great day with those more often than not. It sounds so simple, but there are some subtleties to keeping the ball in play. Especially notice the height and speed of shot that is their favorite and avoid hitting that one. Every shot has some risk associated with it, so if you are expecting to make 100% of your low-risk shots, then you have an unreasonable expectation.

The numbered paragraphs below give you some reasonable expectations and objectives for your match that will help you at least to not beat yourself. Until you have mastered most of what is below, I do not recommend that you move on to more complex strategies and tactics. Here you will see the rationale for allowing for some errors, because every shot has a risk/reward ratio. The following progression of strategies and tactics move from low risk/low reward to high risk/high reward ratios.

Tactics that Support the Strategy "Get and Keep the Ball in Play"

First Serve Percentage

Your first serve percentage is still the #1 factor in deciding the outcome of your match. No matter what your strategy is, a high first serve percentage is part of that. Since the serve is the single most taxing shot in the game that you regularly hit, you will save quite a bit of mental and emotional energy by developing a reliable first serve. If need be, aim for the very center of the service box and 3 feet inside the service line for the safest possible target.

Players sometimes don't realize that when you make your first serve, you actually serve fewer serves, thus keeping you fresh for a longer period in the match. Additionally, it is nearly universal that players win a higher percentage of points when they make their first serve, than when they make their second serve.

There is also a psychological aspect of getting your first serve in, as opponents generally are less ready to attack your first serve, than they are second serve. Opponents become more confident, hopeful and aggressive when returning second serves.

If you make your first serve, you will never double fault.

However; there is a limiting factor when it comes to high serve percentage. Your first serve could become a non-aggressive shot for the sake of trying to make much more than 70% of your serves in play. If you settle for a slightly lower first serve percentage, you will be able to put a little more on you first – you may enjoy less pressure and be able to hit a more effective serve. Some players are blessed with plenty of power and often have serves that cannot be returned very easily, so a serve percentage around 60% can still very effective. Players lacking power, will want to make their serves in the court around 70% of the time, but it's important for them to do all they can to use some power, vary spins, or go for various placements to keep the opponent off balance. Many players unwittingly place their serve into the opponents' forehand every time, because they have made no thought of doing anything else. However, if you are a fairly new player, simply start by getting the first serve in the box, even at the risk of it going to the opponent's forehand.

To show the difference in how serves can vary in effectiveness, consider the two extremes: the power player, and the player who may lack some power, but has a wide variety of serve spins and placements. There was a well noted player who lacked power on his serve, but was very fast around the court. Over much of his career he served 70% first serves in the court, and won 60% of those points. Let's call that an effectiveness quotient of .42 when you multiply the two together. Another noted player who served 50% of first serves in play won 80% of the points for an effectiveness of .40. You can make an argument that the player with less power was more effective. What he lacked was the ability to hit a big serve and erase a break point at a big moment. It's really a great idea to consult with a coach to find out which player are you, and what do they recommend for you to pursue for your ultimate best game.

When I have a player who is capable of hitting big serves, but they hold back for whatever reason, I make it my first task to help them unleash what may be the be most effective part of their game. One particularly difficult problem is a player who is a afraid to take risks, but has been blessed with incredible power potential. If that is you, I would strongly recommend that you learn to play fearlessly, and again, seek coaching to find ways to play the power game with intelligence, and in an effective way, so that you can keep the ball in play. You should know that if you are blessed with great power, you ought not to obsess about keeping the ball in play, because the best offensive players in tennis also have a high tolerance for making more errors than more conservative players.

Return of Serve Percentage

Make your opponent work hard to win their service game. You can create a cumulative effect of stress that increases as the match goes on for them. One key element of making your opponent work hard to hold serve is to return 80% of all serves coming to you. It's much more important to make your opponent play the next ball after the serve than it is to hit an occasional winner. This is when you want to avoid making any unnecessary errors on returns. You don't have to hit the ball back hard, you simply need to get it in play. Some great players are well noted for returning incredibly fast serves, by simply putting their racket out and tapping it back, using the power on the incoming serve as all that is needed to send it back into play.

The safest option for getting the ball back in play is to attempt to strike the ball right back at the server, because hitting it back the same direction makes it much easier to time your shot. Also, when you aim down the middle of the court, you can miss your target by 13.5 feet and it will still be in the court. Once you find you can return serve without a lot of difficulty, then you can steer the majority deep crosscourt, while sometimes going for a bit more angle or surprise the server with an occasional down the line return. Keep your focus on making the returns; if you are going for too much, you are letting the server off the hook with easy point wins. A good guideline is that you can attempt to miss only one return per service game. Once you have missed a second return, it's a great idea to become more conservative, in order to make it tough on the opponent.

As you advance in levels, a more aggressive return game becomes important. The idea here is not to award the server a free point, by missing your return serve. A good mantra to hold in your mind is "make them play". This means that they should have to hit at least two shots or more to win a point. If you do not return serve well, your only hope of winning is to get lucky stringing a few returns together, and hope for a double fault or two, and maybe winning tiebreakers. The best players in the world are always accomplished serve returners.

Movement to the Return

It has been said that 80% of serves will land within one step of where you are returning. With those 80% coming within one step, strive to hit close to 100% of those back, you won't make them all, but have a mindset that you can. 20% of serves will be two or more steps away, so work to hit at least 50% of those back. That may mean some lunging and stretching to get a racket on the ball at times, but two quick steps and you might find it's not that hard to bunt them back. Note: going through a proper warm up is one of the subtle factors that will help you on your return as you prepare for the wild twists and turns you will need in order to make some of these shots. Future eBooks will cover this topic more thoroughly. If your opponent has a monstrous serve, you must strive to make them play more shots, while conceding that some of those serves are just too tough. Be emotionally flexible and give credit to your opponent for having a strong serve.

Note: While I absolutely forbid doing this in any kind of sanctioned play, I have been known to say in a social match with a friend "Wow, that's a great serve. How do you do that?", knowing fully that if they stop to think about how they do it, then its likely they wont serve as well after that. As a coach and friend, I want to make sure that players experience what that kind of gamesmanship can do to your game, so that you can protect yourself from it in the future. When people have tried that same tactic on me, I answer "I don't know how I do it, but here comes another one!". Players who use gamesmanship are trying to get you off your game, and if they can succeed at that, then they can make it more difficult for you to keep the ball in play.

Finally, be a keen observer of patterns that your opponent uses. Do they have a certain place they serve for the first point? For example, at 30- 15 or 15-30, do they have a serve or placement they like? More importantly do they have a serve they use often on break point or game point? When you start to tune into a pattern you can then react better when you recognize the same serve coming. Knowing where they often serve and/or prefer to serve, you can change your positioning to cover those much better. Sometimes you can take a position to try to force them to hit another serve. Some opponents are so well trained to hit their second serve only to the backhand that if you move far enough over that you can hit a forehand. This may render them helpless, and may miss a serve or be less effective when going outside their comfort zone.

The former math teacher in me says "If you make 90% in play out of the 80% that are within one step, and 50% in play out of the 20% that are two more more steps away, that's 72 and 10, and you will have returned 82% of the serves". Make the server play!

Deep Shots in a Rally

Once the rally has begun, when you hit the ball directly down the middle, you can miss by 13.5 feet and you will still not hit the ball wide. When you aim deep crosscourt, you also gain 4.5 more feet to hit into as opposed to down the line shots. Hitting down the line gives you 78 feet, but crosscourt the diagonal length of the court is 82.5 Feet. Going for a little height and depth makes gravity your friend by helping to the ball in the court. Trying to rip an impressive, but less effective lower percentage shot just barely over the net can make gravity your enemy - making the ball go into the net. It has been disproven the value of the net being lower in the middle, as the net is further from you on a crosscourt shot than it is on a down the line shot. When you are playing deep shots, It's a far better surprise to have a ball land in, that you thought was going out, than to have it hit the net when you thought it might go over. When you are aiming for deep shots, you will pay more attention to the deep part of the court, then you will avoid the net quite often, because your eyes and mind are not focused on it as an obstacle to overcome, because you have shifted your focus to locations further in the court.

Up to a certain level of play 75% of errors by the average player go into the net. If you focus on hitting the ball a bit higher over the net, it will result in fewer errors. You have no chance of your opponent hitting the shot back if it is in the net, but, you do have a chance of them playing a long ball. Your errors will decrease. When I am training players for the first time to keep their balls deep in the court, and I ask them to hit the ball out long, they discover that its actually harder than it looks.

Hitting your groundstrokes deep crosscourt is the way to build your points. Two books come to mind that you can read to support this notion. Dr. Allen Fox's "Think to Win" and Paul Wardlaw's "Pressure Tennis" have been quite helpful to me personally and my players when it comes to winning more matches. I recommend them highly. You will find some great drills in Wardlaw's book. I see those books as more detailed studies for those that want to be very successful Tennis Players or coaches.

Essentially, you will build your points with crosscourt shots, showing patience, waiting for a short ball or a down the line ball, then you can attack with a down the line shot. The deeper you can safely hit the ball crosscourt, the more likely you are to draw a weak reply that you can attack. What constitutes a weak reply is predicted on your ability to take advantage of opportunities and ability to recognize them.

Know Your Game and Your Future Game

It's wise to have a long term plan for what kind of player you want to be. Your style should be a reflection not only of your growth in character, but match your physique and special abilities. Some people are more powerful and explosive, others are more cautious and have better fine motor control. If you are the explosive player, (yes, of course you do have to keep most balls in play), you have much more to gain from playing a higher risk game than your counterpart who has better fine motor control. Players neurotically use the phrase "Be more consistent", not realizing what there true application of that phrase really means. What they should be thinking is "never miss"; everyone misses at some point, players shouldn't obsess over missed shots. Player should instead be working toward playing intelligent Tennis using calculated risk, realizing that really almost any shot can be missed. On the other hand, if you are missing shots often, that can easily be made, then you definitely want to check in with a Tennis Professional to help you with that.

As you gain experience, and are ready to move beyond getting and keeping the ball in play, start developing a plan for building new tactics into your game, at the right time. I have seen quite a few players who were taught to play according to a coach or academy's philosophy, even though it was a 'cookie cutter' approach. Are you a cookie? NO! So learn and train according to your strengths, and learn to mitigate your weaknesses. It's not likely to happen if you are trying to learn to play like someone who had different strengths.

\#

A Different Approach on Second Serve Return

On first serve return you generally want to make the other player play another shot. On second serve you want to be on the attack. However, you don't want to miss more than 1 out of 5 attacking shots.

There is also a fairly large amount of spontaneity that comes with attempting to return serve. When your opponent hits a strong serve that goes right into your 'wheel house', then you may be able to crush it, as a high percentage play. Sometimes pathetic second serves can travel so slowly that timing the shot becomes an issue, and it's possible to botch an attempt to attack. Don't be discouraged.

How well you make your opponent play, and how well you attack second serves are the second most important factor in a match. If the first serve puts someone ahead in a point, then a great return equalizes it. If a second serve puts the player in a neutral position, then a great return gives the returner the lead in the point.

On the Day of The Match

When you warm up, focus mainly on rhythm and placement. It's pretty simple advice.

Mental Skills: Keeping the Ball in Play

When you are playing a "keep the ball in" strategy, there are two main mental skills you will want to focus on from point to point. The first skill to develop is paying attention to your effort level, maintaining as close to 100% as you can, and notice any dips in effort. Keeping the ball in play is also known as "The High Effort Game", so it's essential to work on that.

Concentration is the other mental skill. Two things that will help your overall concentration are:

1. Allowing your eyes to rest for a few moments between points.

2. Using much of the 90 seconds changeover to rest your concentration.

When you attempt to concentrate in every moment of a match you will certainly become quite fatigued. Resting your mind for moments at a time will prolong your ability to concentrate over a longer period.

Pressure Opponent's Movement

The player who has the ability to control the depth of their shot has quite an advantage over the player that cannot control depth. With today's new rackets which feature less dense string patterns, the 'angle of deflection' from a Tennis racket is much higher than it was in the past. This will aid a player tremendously at hitting more spin, having a higher trajectory over the net, and thus more depth. The question for that player is, can they sufficiently adjust the angle of their racket head at contact to also hit shorter and sharper angled shots? This is a great subject for which to consult a Tennis Professional in your area.

Tactics at the Top of the List for Pressuring Movement

Keep the ball as deep as possible on every shot during a rally, until the opponent hits a shorter ball. Keeping the ball deep during the rally, keeps your opponent pushed further back in the court, making it very difficult for them to hurt you with their shot. Although, there are times when some low percentage shots can be made by the opponent. Don't get discouraged if your opponent can win 10% of the points while pushed way back in the court.

When both players are keeping the ball deep, of course there is some risk of an error long, however, that is an acceptable error to make any time the ball is only out by a foot or two. If you are missing by much more than that its time for a change. You can only learn to control the ball deep in the court, by risking the occasional out ball. If many balls are deep and you are losing, then it's probably time to go back to 'keeping the ball in play'.

The best definition I have seen for a deep shot is one that lands in the second half of the large rectangle. If you have seen a 60' court, the line that exists marking 60' is perfect, so focus on hitting beyond that line. The 60' mark is 9' in from the baseline. If you keep your ball in the last nine feet of the court you will be very tough to beat. This will keep your opponent moving sideways or even backwards to hit the ball. A fairly large percentage of the time, when two players engage in a very deep rally, and one of them is the first to unintentionally hit short, the other player gains a very large advantage in the point. That player can now move forward and will have at least two different options of where to hit the next ball to put their opponent under pressure.

Directional Shots Pressure Opponent's Movement

Whenever I coach at match at any level, a constant piece of advice that I give my players is 'Build your points with cross court shots.' Crosscourt play gives you not only more court for which you to hit into by 4.5 feet, but also has the potential of pushing your opponent much further back and to the side of the court than down the line shots. Dr. Allen Fox explained in his book "Think to Win" how the notion of 'Hit it where they aren't' is not a good idea if the down the line shot seems open, just because your opponent is not standing in that spot. When you go for a down the line shot that does not significantly pressure your opponent, that allows your opponent to hit the ball crosscourt and immediately pressure your movement. When you rally crosscourt patiently, you may find a time to hit a slightly more aggressive angle, which can tilt the point in your favor. In the meantime, the amount of moving you will need to recover to an ideal for the potential shots of your opponent will be less.

When it comes to the adage "Control, Hurt, Finish", controlling the point is where the crux of this strategy lies. When you find yourself in a rally, both players are attempting to maintain control of the rally. Crosscourt shots help you to maintain control of the rally. When one player hits the ball short, or goes down the line without hurting the other player, then that player has a prime opportunity to Hurt you with their shot. If you are disciplined in regard to building points with deep crosscourt play, you will find that you can control the points better, and your opponent will more often be the one that gives you a chance to hurt them with an angle or a down the line shot on your terms.

In actual practice you may find that the system of Control, Hurt, Finish may end at any time. In the midst of controlling points, your opponent may miss their shot. While attempting a shot to hurt your opponent, you may 'accidentally' hit a winner.

Depth Control for Advancing Players

Advanced players may have the ability to hit a lower shorter shot intentionally and with enough directional control, that it puts their opponent off balance. One example of this would be a Roger Federer short slice shot to an opponent with a two handed backhand, keeping the ball low, really forcing that opponent to run forward and bend low to make the shot. When Andre Agassi switched to a strategy primarily based on keeping the ball very deep in the court and his opponent moving around at the back, he experienced very lengthy periods at the top of the ATP game. Rafael Nadal has been quoted as saying when asked about his strategy in a match, "I hit a lot of heavy topspin deep to the backhand, pretty simple, no?" One principle to observe is that when a player combines extreme athleticism with great technique, or even unique technique, they create a match up problem for their opponent that allows them to play a fairly simple strategy.

A deep serve will keep your opponent pushed back as much as possible. Short serves can create easier opportunities for the opponent to gain the offensive in a point immediately.

Shot combinations that feature one deep ball and one shorter ball and vice versa are one of the best staples for a winning game. When you are able to control and vary the depth of your shots the amount of pressure you can put on your opponent improves dramatically. By doing this you introduce a different element - your opponent must move diagonally up or back for the shot. One classic shot combination that I teach to all my players is to hit a topspin shot on a short angle that lands near the service line on one side of the court, followed by a deep shot to the opposite corner, or vice versa. It does not matter whether you have intentionally or accidentally hit the first shot in the sequence, you can follow up with the second shot and you will find you have taken an opportunity to create a great shot combination.

Keeping the ball very low and short can be a great strategy against a heavy topspin player, tall players, or those who hit very flat balls, but you must have extremely effective slice and flat shots to make it work.

On the Day of the Match

Warm up by hitting the ball out long. For a few minutes in your practice at the beginning you and your partner can work to hit the ball 3 to 5 feet out, then shift to hitting toward the baseline and finally a few feet inside. Make sure you get great length on shots in the warm up, as you may have some difficulty in the match if you tighten up at all.

Mental Skill: Pressuring Your Opponent's Movement

Eliminate a fear of hitting long. Learn to very much despise hitting the first short ball in a rally. Have something that you tell yourself if your ball goes long. I like "At least I am being aggressive with my depth" or "OK, now I just need to hit it 3 feet shorter for a shot with great depth" or something along those lines. One great benefit of this depth seeking is that you will lose sight of the net, and very few balls will go into the net because of the shift in your focus.

Also, come to the realization that you might not execute your shot combinations perfectly in a point. That might mean that you have to start over in the point. Also be ready to capitize on accidental shots that become the first shot of a combination, and smartly make the second shot in that combination. Always be alert to opportunities.

Strategy: Pressure your Opponent's Time and Space

Pressuring your opponent's time and space can be done in different ways. You can start with the serve, and continue in a rally, sometimes you can do it with a return of serve, but the most dramatic form is approaching the net. Still another great way to pressure your opponent's time and space is to bring them to the net on your terms. The speed or the location of your shot can pressure your opponent. Your movement forward changing the tempo of the rally can also put pressure on your opponent. Your forward movement can also have the effect of shrinking the space that your opponent can hit past you. In this chapter we will mainly focus on the serve and rally aspects of taking time away from your opponent.

You can use your serve to take away time and space, since the shortest distance between two points is a straight line, your serve will arrive faster to your opponent when you hit it right at them.

Tactics: Pressure Opponent's Time and Space

This pressures your opponent in two ways. One, they have less time to react because the distance is shorter. Two, you force them to make a decision very quickly as to whether to take it as a forehand or backhand and then also to pick to which target they want to hit. Advanced players can serve to either side of the line of decision and thus force the opponent to make tougher decisions. If your serve is too slow or it always goes slightly to the forehand side, this will not be as effective as faster serves that are directed at the body.

Another benefit of serving into the body, is that you cause you opponent to first respect and maybe fear that serve, which can leave them slightly hesitant to move to corner balls, because they worry about the body serve. This way you can be more effective with serves wide or down the middle of the court. A word of caution is that some players are very well trained to get out of the way of the ball hit at them moving to hit a big forehand.

Subtle and Obvious Tactics to Pressure Time and Space

I have heard it said, "playing aggressively does not necessarily mean hitting hard, it means moving forward". On return of serve, standing at the baseline, or even slightly inside the baseline can give you the opportunity to put your opponent under time pressure, but that is predicated on how good the incoming serve might be. You may even find yourself inching in closer to the net. Caution: No matter how weak your opponent's serve is, I never recommend standing any further forward than halfway inside the large rectangle behind the service line. If you are too close to the service box, you are in danger of being pushed back by the serve, if it lands deep in the service box.

There was a junior player I trained for a while and I would test his ability to understand the game. He and I would play points, and I would ask him questions about the pivotal moment in a point where it was won, lost, or something took control of it. In an attempt to help him discover how to put time pressure on an opponent: I would rally a few balls back, then I would quickly step forward a few feet for the next ball, changing the rhythm of the rally, putting him under a subtle time pressure. He would them miss his shot or hit something weak for me to capitalize on for an attack. After the point I would ask him "What happened in that point?" He had a number of answers as I continued to use this same tactic against him. He felt he had done something wrong. When I explained that I had changed the rhythm of the rally and that he should look to see if I had changed my position, as that would affect the amount of time he would have to recover for his next shot. Once he made the adjustment, it was much more difficult for me to victimize him with that tactic. He then was better able to defend, but he used the same tactic against me and others.

Coming to the net can be simple or it can be complex. The more you work on your technique and make your trips to the net a complex problem for your opponent, the better off you will be. At the very least If you learn to hit a low and deep approach shot and can come forward for one good volley to finish a point, then you have enough net game to pressure your opponent. Up to a 4.0 level of play you either need a very good approach shot, or a very good volley. Once you want to climb to 4.5 and above and want to play the net, you must have a very good approach and volley, and the ability to hit more than one volley to win the point. Also, when you have a reliable overhead, then your confidence at the net will soar.

Let's cover some of the basics of coming to the net. First, come in on a ball that would be easy to run forward immediately after hitting the ball. If hitting the approach shot forces you to really stop or even move back slightly, it's not the right ball for you to come to the net. Also the incoming ball should not pull you off balance or a be a ball that you may have trouble controlling. Your goal is to hit a ball deep down the line, and move right inside the service line. Again, see a coach for the specifics of what is realistic for you and your game.

I define a deep ball as one that lands in the second half of the large rectangle, so essentially in the last nine feet of the court. You don't have to hit the baseline, although the closer it goes to the baseline, the better of an approach it will be. Additionally if it's fairly close to the sideline on your down the line shot, that's great, but it's far more important for it to be deep.

When approaching on your forehand side, I recommend hitting the ball with a minimal amount of topspin, just enough for it to land it, but not so much that it lands short and jumps up. Less topspin will not only help you gain more depth in the court, but give you a lower ball with more speed, all of which together puts more pressure on your opponent. You may also accidentally hit a winner, or force an error outright from your opponent, either of those is great, but continue to be ready to volley. Too many times in my life I have seen players come to the net, believing that their approach was too good and the opponent will not get there, they relax. The opponent then returns the ball and because the approaching player lost focus for a moment, they miss the volley. So be sure that you are there, present and ready, for anything until you are certain the point is over.

In 2015 groundbreaking research was divided out from the statistical data from the US Open. Shared by BrainGameTennis.com's Craig O'Shannessy, players won 62% of all net approaches to the backhand side of their opponents.

Coming the net suddenly forces your opponent to have to hit a great shot, immediately. Even if in the short term the opponent can handle that, over time the repeated challenge can wear them down and have a cumulative effect of pressure on them. Additionally, a passing shot thats easy at 15-love for them, becomes much more difficult for them when a game or set is on the line. While I don't necessarily prescribe to 'playing according to the score', having a set play to apply more pressure on pivotal points can be a positive factor for success.

Before we wrap up this section, I want to include another tactic for pressuring the opponent's time and space, which is to bring your opponent to the net on your terms, not theirs. Some people you play seem allergic to the net, and will only come to the net to shake hands at the end of a match. Others love the net and want to come forward as much as they can, but on their terms.

2nd Best Pressure Tactic

Bringing the Opponent Up on Your Terms

Against the 'Net Allergen' player, you can hit intentionally very short shots that pull them forward off balance. Keep doing this until they are forced to come in and then pass them or lob them. This is easier said than done, but you can see that it would require your ability to control the depth of your shots and described in another strategy.

It may seem odd to bring the player who likes the net forward, but if you have them coming in on your terms, then they will not be as comfortable coming forward, and you can gain an edge. Here is the best example: Raymond, the #1 player at a high school where I was coaching, who had been a fairly high ranked junior and was about equivalent to a 4.0 level player, was facing a senior who had been all-league the year before and was bigger, faster, stronger, and loved coming to the net. Very early in the set Raymond found himself down a break, but he shifted his focus to making sure the net player had to stretch for the first volley, so that he could open up space on the other side for a passing shot. My player broke serve, and won a very narrow set in a tiebreaker. For the second set, Raymond focused on hitting short balls to the sides of the court, and not down the middle. The opponent was then forced to come in with a sort of zig zag movement which increased the distance and slowed him down due to the direction change necessary. Raymond broke serve twice in the set to win 6-3 and come out with a convincing win, from what may have been a very tight match, simply because he made the net player play according to his terms.

On the Day of the Match

Maybe you don't need to put pressure on your opponent's time and space to win today's match. That's OK, but sometimes it's the only way to make an impression on some types of players. Be sure to take a few balls early by stepping inside the court to time your shot properly. Attempting to execute this strategy without practicing the timing on the court surface on which you are playing the match today can lead to some unnecessary errors.

Mental Skills: Pressuring Time and Space

When coming forward, be the aggressor, take charge of the point. Be ready to roll the dice, gamble and win 65% or more of the points. Maybe coming to the net is your only way to win 50% or more of the points, so be ready continue. As for bringing the other player up, be mentally prepared to hit softer lower shots that land around the service line or even a bit shorter. This is a great reason to warm up in the short court to practice those types of placements. Also, realize that when you shift to this strategy in a match, you might make an error or two in the early going as you figure out the timing of the shot

Break Up Your Opponent's Rhythm

Bill Tilden in "Match Play and Spin of the Ball" said, something to the effect of "Every ball should be struck with some type of intentional spin". So whether you choose to hit the ball with nearly the exact spin every time, or go for a very wide variety of spins, if you do so intentionally then you have it nailed. Your intention should be based on what you see in your opponent. However, if you have not thought much about this then you are missing out on a very effective strategy that can change the outcome of a match. Tilden also said "Find out which shot your opponent hates the most... and know which shot is your opponent's favorite", again I am paraphrasing. Once you know your opponent's least favorite shot, whether its high topspin, low slice, or a very fast flat ball with almost no spin, you can use that knowledge to set chances to hit that way when you really want a point, especially if you are down in a game, or have a game point. Knowing the opponent's strength helps you to avoid it, and it might be that they love when you give them just enough spin so they can take it at a certain height. I know that for my own game, when players hit me a certain amount of topspin, that allowed me to tee off on my groundstrokes, hitting more winners. HIgher or lower, and I would have to work my way to net in order be be more effective. If you can spin it differently to give the opponent a ball higher, lower, wider, or tighter to their body to take them away from their ideal contact point, you can greatly diminish their effectiveness. Make sure you are comfortable and confident with all the spins, before you decide to try them in a match for the first time

Selected Tactics for Breaking Up Opponent's Rhythm

1. Slice shot that elicits a short return, followed by a heavy topspin angled shot.

2. Varying topspin, slice, topspin shots can get your opponent out of rhythm.

3. A variety of topspins heavy, medium, to almost flat, to change the way the ball 'jumps' to the opponent. Also when hitting topspin you can attack the balls from different angles to create subtle differences in how the ball jumps.

4. Hitting no two shots alike can really wreck your opponent's rhythm. More on that later.

5. Serve with different types of spin by attacking the ball at different angles. 6. Serves that are spun above the 45 degree plane, or from 7 o'clock to 1 o'clock will have a very different effect than a ball struck at 8 o'clock to 2 o'clock. See a seasoned Tennis Professional if this is not clear to you. This not so subtle change is due to the difference in how the bottom of the ball is spinning when it makes contact with the ground.

If you use spin expertly, you can convince your opponent that they are having a bad day. Sadly, you may not gain acknowledgement for having played well, your opponent, their coaches and family will blame them for losing, while you know the real truth.

On the Day of the Match

Figure out which spin you want to start with in your warm up. Find a way that works for you. I like to start with moderate topspin, then slice, then alternate slice and topspin. From there Hit a moderate topspin, followed by heavy topspin and minimal topspin, just enough to keep the ball in the court.

Mental Skill: Disrupting Rhythm

Acceptance of a few errors will be important if you are going to change up your spins quite often. You will have to accept a few miss hits, and some occasional bad choices, and some ineffective shots. First, accept your error, then quickly think about how you can do better then next time in that same situation.

Power: the Final Strategy to Master, unless... Simple tactics for the power game

If you are going to be a power player, then you must work very hard to have impeccable timing on a wide variety of shots coming your way. I have seen Andre Agassi's coach working with him and giving Agassi every kind of ball imaginable. Agassi hit them all very hard, relentlessly. On the other hand you will also need to be able to play some defensive shots, because when you give your opponent power to work with, then they will also hit some offensive shots. You will want to be able to neutralize their powerful shot with a nice slice, a lob or a looping shot, before you go right back on the attack.

On the Day of the Match

Set the tone early. By the end of your pre-match warm up you will want to be hitting the ball confidently as hard as you can with 'controlled aggression'. All the power in the world will not help you if your ball is out.

Set the tone in the match. Hit the first serve of the match as hard as you can, if it goes in, do it again, if you are serving out of your mind, keep going. I have had players play magically on a given day and simply pummel the other player into oblivion, this is not a time for thinking. Carry on! However, if you miss that first serve, or you get derailed from your power game plan, consider adding some spin to your shots to keep them in, but only apply enough spin, so that you don't completely lose your aggression. Should spin not help, then you can focus on keeping the ball deep, being very patient and waiting for a short ball before becoming aggressive again. If that's not working hit some deep/short, short/deep combinations to elicit a weak reply. Do you see where I am headed? If you have built your power game on top of these foundations that come first, then if your power game is off for a day, you can fall back on other tactics and still find yourself with opportunities to finish points with power. With no foundation previous, I guess you just have a bad day and lose. So...

If all else fails focus on deep crosscourt, and it really may come back to simply running around and making one more shot. Let's hope it never comes back to that.

Mental Skill: Power Tennis

Commitment to your game plan and your development as a power player means you stay committed to it as your "A game" even if you make a few consecutive errors, but if you find yourself down a set and a break, then you may consider a strategic shift. However, do not abandon your game plan simply because you made a few errors, even a few in a row. Power Tennis means higher risk, and you have to continue taking risks to play your game.

The Best and Most Tiring Ways to Win

The best way to win is to overpower your opponent. It can also be the easiest way to lose. Sometimes even in a warm up you can see that your opponent can't handle your power. So play powerfully. It's the best way to win, because the points are shorter, and you expend less energy in winning the match, unless you fail to play with controlled aggression, because then you will make an inordinate amount of errors, making things more difficult for yourself. So, if you are winning games easily, continue on, but if you have a second match on the day, and you are making more than 2 errors per game, and games are going to deuce, you may want to play slightly differently.

This completely backfires, when power feeds right into your opponents' strengths, they love pace, and have a way of beating you with it. Also, if you are getting overpowered and are losing a set, either ramp it up, or switch to another mode of play. Some players will use all of the pace you provide, and simply return it with none, or turn it into massive spin.

Second best way to win is to keep your opponent under constant pressure to move. Using shot combinations that rarely allow your opponent to set up for their shot on time and in balance, will feed you a steady stream of weaker shots, and you can build your game on attacking in various ways the short or floating balls that come your way. I recommend that you build the strength of your point on crosscourt play, going for greater angles when the opportunity arises. If you continue to build your points with initial crosscourt shots, your opponent will move more and you will move less.

Time pressure with court position and change of pace. When you move forward or intentionally hit a slightly faster ball in a rally, you can take over the point. Sometimes this is subtle and sometimes not very subtle at all. Generally it's true that if your opponent is much faster on court than you, it will be good for you to move a bit closer in to keep them under time pressure. Faster opponents generally do not feel a lot of movement pressure, so you want to instead take away their time. This can also include coming to the net occasionally.

Disrupting the opponents rhythm can work to support one of the three above strategies. Either you can use this strategy over the course of a full match, or you can use it as a way to get your opponent off their game until you can return to your own "A game". Sometimes you play a someone who loves this type of play, and they will quickly use it against you by playing it better. Some people really love to be very creative with their shot making and the more you junk things up, the more you play into their hands so be careful.

On a day when all else has failed, running around hitting one more ball in the court can win you a match. Through sheer will and competitive instincts, counterpunching through a match to win can be very courageous. As a way of life, or a career, it can lead to injury, and overuse. Every match will be difficult. You will find it harder and hard to put opponents away. Those will more aggressive games will always have a chance of being ON, and can beat you when they play in the zone. You however will rarely if ever beat yourself. I strongly recommend that you begin to branch out and work to develop some of the skills shown above so that this will someday be your B or C game. There have been times as a player and a coach, that all else was failing and the only chance of winning was to run 6 miles for the victory. You have to do what you have to do!

When to Change Strategy and What to Expect

Strategic shifts are not easy to pull off, as there is a period of adjustment. So whether you are using your A game or B game, you might want to pick the one that you believe has the best chance against today's opponent. Winning on the day and in the match is always the most important consideration of the day, using all the tools at your disposal. When making a shift toward building more tools in your game, in the short term you will find that you lose a match that you may have won previously. When you manage it best, you can experience those losses in a practice match situation, and not a live tournament or team match situation. One of the lost pieces in the over programming of a tennis player is that practice match, or a friendly match just for the love of the game.

How to Build New Strategy into your Game

I often tell my students that there are five steps to truly building a new stroking weapon, or tactic to support a strategy.

Step One: Take a Lesson on the technique or tactic. There may be some closed skill drilling, and some repetitive drilling.

Step Two: Live ball drilling featuring that same skill or tactic.

Step Three: Point play competition where the skill or tactic is required or rewarded.

Step Four: Practice matches where the tactic or technique is stressed much more than the winning of the match. Wait until confidence and mastery come about before using it in...

Step Five: using what you have learned in a lesser tournament, so that you can decide whether you will also use it against the best competition you will face.

Now that you have fully bought into this progression as a framework, I hope you are not disappointed when I turn them on their head. I hope you understand that in order to climb to the top of game and do what is best, you need other supporting structures based on smart Tennis. So now, let's turn this thing completely upside down. From this list of five ways to win, I hope you have one strong one match strategy, in which you are very confident, and two others that you are comfortable in playing. If you can play all five, you will be quite successful, be careful not to overthink your matches.

Developing a Long Term Approach to Playing Style

Wherever you find yourself along this continuum of playing styles, it's wise to be thoughtful about your plan for the future of your game. What will you need to become to play the way you want to play? My own transformation from counterpunching baseline player to full time serve and volleyer happened overnight. Only on very special days where my opponent was overmatched or hitting right into my wheel house, did I ever play a power game. I did however rack up more wins than losses against players more powerful than myself, by using all the guile described in these pages. Even more importantly, the players I have coached have benefitted greatly from the fact that I learned from past mistakes so that I could help them at a younger age find their A, B and maybe their C game. My hope is that you will experience the great fun that comes from using sound strategies and find similar or better success than my people.

This ends this section on basic strategy. My goal with this is to give you a sample of the foundation upon which the rest of the books will be built, including the print book which will be ready in early 2015.

Made in the USA
Las Vegas, NV
01 November 2022

58578982R00021